Franklin Watts
12a Golden Square
London W1

Franklin Watts Australia
14 Mars Road
Lane Cove
N.S.W. 2066

ISBN: 0 86313 670 2

Design: Edward Kinsey

Typesetting: Tradespools Ltd,
Frome

Printed by G. Canale, Turin, Italy

The Publishers would like to
thank the Lal family and all other
people shown in this book.

Bhai Bhagwant Singh is Granthi
of the Gurdwara in Shepherd's
Bush, London.

Note: Many of the photographs
in this book originally appeared
in 'My Belief: I am a Sikh'

SIKH

Jenny Wood

Photographs: Chris Fairclough
Consultant: Bhai Bhagwant Singh

Franklin Watts
London/New York/Sydney/Toronto

These people are Sikhs.
They follow the Sikh religion.

Sikhs follow
the teachings of the Gurus
who said there is One True God.
The Sikh Holy Book
sets down rules for living.

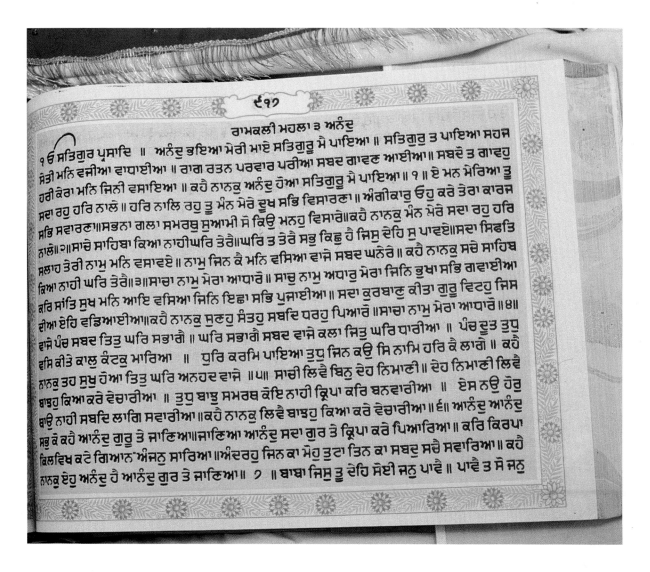

The Sikh Holy Book is called
Guru Granth Sahib.
It was written in a special script
by the fifth Guru, Guru Arjan.

9

Parents explain the meaning
of the five Sikh symbols.
These are worn or carried to show
that a person is a Sikh.

The five symbols are the bangle,
the comb, the pair of shorts,
the sword, and the hair and turban.

Sikh men do not cut their hair.
The turban keeps their hair
in place. It is an insult to try
to remove a Sikh's turban.

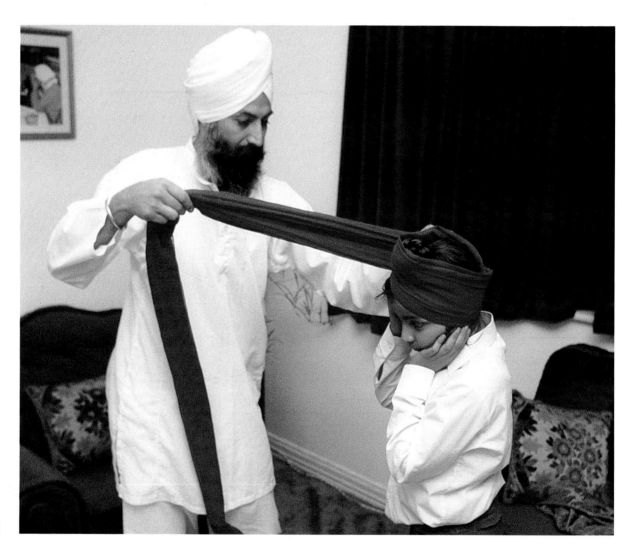

The turban is a long piece of cloth about 5 metres long. It is wound round the head from left to right. The ends are then tucked in.

Most Sikh men wear
European clothes, but always
with a turban. White turbans,
shirts and trousers are worn
on special occasions.

Sikh women sometimes wear
a long dress called a sari.
Most wear loose trousers
under a long tunic.

This is a Sikh temple.
It is called a Gurdwara.
The yellow flag shows that
it is a holy place for Sikhs.

Every week, Sikhs gather in
the temple to worship.
Before going inside,
they take off their shoes
and leave them in the porch.

Everyone worships together.
Men usually sit on the right
and women on the left.

Before the service begins,
each person kneels in front of
the Sikh Holy Book.
This is kept on a special platform
in the temple.

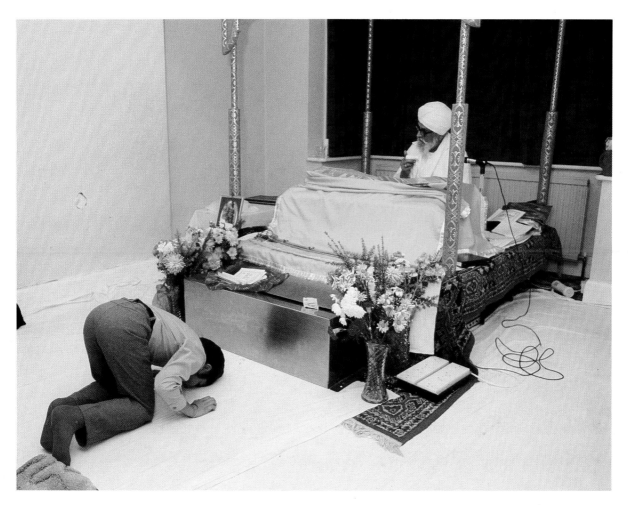

If there is a special ceremony at the Gurdwara, everyone helps to prepare the food.

Favourite foods are chapatis
and vegetable curries.
Many Sikhs do not eat meat.

Today, there is a wedding
in the Gurdwara.
All the relations and friends
of the bride and groom are there.

During the ceremony,
the bride and groom are given
garlands of flowers and money.

Music is played at all the important
festivals and ceremonies.
Sometimes everyone joins in,
singing verses from the Holy Book.

Festivals are a time for Sikhs
to remember their Gurus.
Baisakhi, celebrated every April,
begins with the Holy Book
being uncovered.

Sikh families like
to spend time together.
They sing and give thanks to God
for the Sikh way of life.

FACTS ABOUT SIKHS

The Sikh religion was begun in north-west India over 500 years ago.

Sikh teachers are called Gurus. Every Sikh learns the teachings of the ten Gurus on which the Sikh faith is based.

The important rules are:
– believing in one God who created everything
– earning an honest living and sharing with others
– not using alcohol, tobacco or drugs
– believing that all people are equal

The five symbols (sometimes called the five Ks) which show that a person is a Sikh are:
– *Kara*, a steel bracelet, to show eternity
– *Kirpan*, a sword, to show strength
– *Kacchehra*, a pair of shorts, to show action and goodness
– *Kesh* and *Keski*, the hair and the turban, to show wisdom
– *Kangha*, a comb to show cleanliness

27

GLOSSARY

Chapatis
A kind of round, flat bread made out of wheat flour.

Guru
A Sikh teacher.

Gurdwara
A Sikh temple. The word means "the place of the Guru".

Holy Book
This is also called the Guru Granth Sahib. It contains the sacred writings of the Sikh Gurus.

Kacchehra
A pair of shorts.

Kangha
A comb.

Kara
A steel bracelet.

Kesh
Hair.

Keski
A turban.

Kirpan
A sword or dagger worn by Sikhs.

INDEX